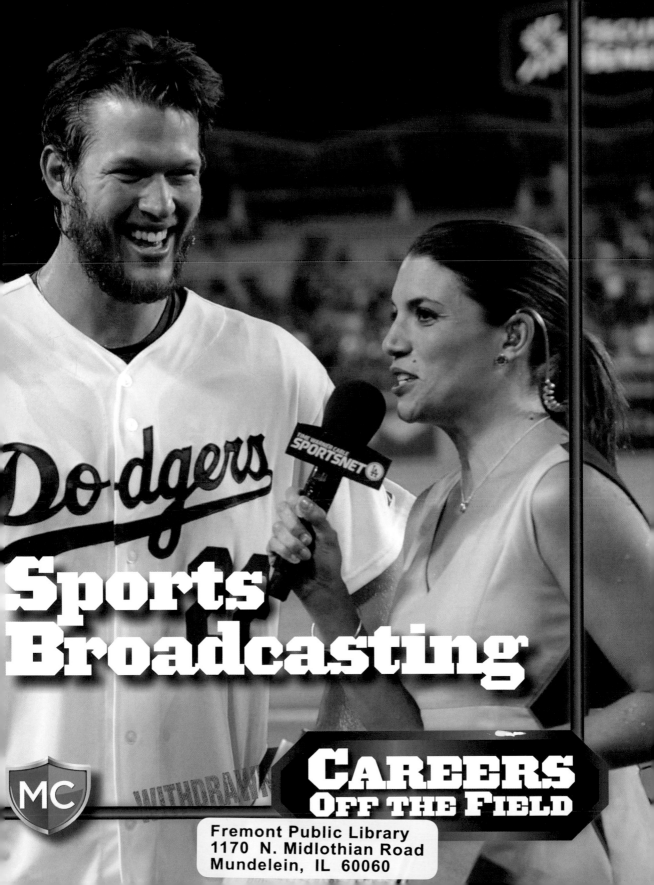

Sports Broadcasting

CAREERS OFF THE FIELD

CAREERS OFF THE FIELD

Sports Broadcasting

By John Walters

Mason Crest
450 Parkway Drive, Suite D
Broomall, PA 19008
www.masoncrest.com

Printed and bound in the United States of America.

Series ISBN: 978-1-4222-3264-4
Hardback ISBN: 978-1-4222-3271-2
EBook ISBN: 978-1-4222-8529-9

First printing
1 3 5 7 9 8 6 4 2

Produced by Shoreline Publishing Group LLC
Santa Barbara, California
Editorial Director: James Buckley Jr.
Designer: Bill Madrid
Production: Sandy Gordon
www.shorelinepublishing.com
Cover photo: Mike Weyerhaeuser/Actionplus/Newscom
Cover: Pitcher Clayton Kershaw of the Los Angeles Dodgers is interviewed on the field by a cable television reporter.

Library of Congress Cataloging-in-Publication Data
Walters, John (John Andrew)
        Sports broadcasting / by John Walters.
                pages cm. -- (Careers off the field)
        Includes bibliographical references and index.
        ISBN 978-1-4222-3271-2 (hardback : alk. paper) -- ISBN 978-1-4222-3264-4 (series : alk. paper) -- ISBN 978-1-4222-8529-9 (ebook) 1. Television broadcasting of sports--Juvenile literature. 2. Radio broadcasting of sports--Juvenile literature. 3. Sportscasters--Juvenile literature. 4. Sports journalism--Juvenile literature. I. Title.
        GV742.3.W357 2016
        070.4'49796--dc23
                        2015011890

CONTENTS

Key Icons to Look For

 Words to Understand: These words with their easy-to-understand definitions will increase the reader's understanding of the text, while building vocabulary skills.

 Sidebars: This boxed material within the main text allows readers to build knowledge, gain insights, explore possibilities, and broaden their perspectives by weaving together additional information to provide realistic and holistic perspectives.

 Research Projects: Readers are pointed toward areas of further inquiry connected to each chapter. Suggestions are provided for projects that encourage deeper research and analysis.

 Text-Dependent Questions: These questions send the reader back to the text for more careful attention to the evidence presented here.

 Series Glossary of Key Terms: This back-of-the-book glossary contains terminology used throughout this series. Words found here increase the reader's ability to read and comprehend higher-level books and articles in this field.

Foreword
By Al Ferrer

So you want to work in sports? Good luck! You've taken a great first step by picking up this volume of CAREERS OFF THE FIELD. I've been around sports professionally—on and off the field, in the front office, and in the classroom—for more than 35 years. My students have gone on to work in all the major sports leagues and for university athletic programs. They've become agents, writers, coaches, and broadcasters. They were just where you are now, and the lessons they learned can help you succeed.

One of the most important things to remember when looking for a job in sports is that being a sports fan is not enough. If you get an interview with a team, and your first sentence is "I'm your biggest fan," that's a kiss of death. They don't want fans, they want pros. Show your experience, show what you know, show how you can contribute.

Another big no-no is to say, "I'll do anything." That makes you a non-professional or a wanna-be. You have to do the research and find out what area is best for your personality and your skills. This book series will be a vital tool for you to do that research, to find out what areas in sports are out there, what kind of people work in them, and where you would best fit in.

That leads to my third point: Know yourself. Look carefully at your interests and skills. You need to understand what you're good at and how you like to work. If you get energy from being around people, then you don't want to be in a room with a computer because you'll go nuts. You want to be in the action, around people, so you might look at sales or marketing or media relations or being an agent. If you're more comfortable being by yourself, then you look at analysis, research, perhaps the numbers side of scouting or recruiting. You have to know yourself.

You also have to manage your expectations. There is a lot of money in sports, but unless you are a star athlete, you probably won't be making much in your early years.

I'm not trying to be negative, but I want to be realistic. I've loved every minute of my life in sports. If you have a passion for sports and you can bring professionalism and quality work—and you understand your expectations—you can have a great career. Just like the athletes we admire, though, you have to prepare, you have to work hard, and you have to never, ever quit.

Series consultant Al Ferrer founded the sports management program at the University of California, Santa Barbara, after an award-winning career as a Division I baseball coach. Along with his work as a professor, Ferrer is an advisor to pro and college teams, athletes, and sports businesses.

Introduction

Words to Understand

depth charts: a listing of football team positions, noting the starters and backups at each position

IFB: Interruptible Foldback (or Feedback)—a device that lets TV producers talk into the ear of on-air broadcasters

It's Saturday, and while most of the country has the day off, Charles Davis (left) rises at dawn. Today, Davis wakes up in Eugene, Oregon, where the biggest college football game of the day, Michigan State at Oregon, will kick off this afternoon. As half of FOX Sports' lead college football broadcast team, Davis and his partner, Gus Johnson, will be calling today's action from Autzen Stadium.

"Everyone has his own routine on game day," says Davis, 50, "and I certainly have mine. It begins with waking up early."

Davis works as a color analyst, while Johnson does play-by-play. You might think of it this way: Johnson's job is to drive the tour bus, and Davis' job is to point out the sights and inform the passengers about what they are seeing. For Davis, who played safety at the University of Tennessee, it is a labor of love.

"I love to talk about college football," he says.

Davis starts this day as he does every game day—by reading a packet of notes. The packet, which is about 15 pages long, is filled with notes and reminders that Davis has compiled. None of the information is specific to today's game.

"For example," says Davis, "I have a line from *The Jungle Book*. It reads, 'The strength of the wolf is the pack, the strength of the pack is the wolf.'"

Davis also keeps a list of synonyms for commonly used words so that, as he says, "I don't say 'great' twenty times per game."

After that ritual is completed, Davis hits the gym to release some anxiety. Then he returns to his hotel room and reads newspaper articles and online stories related to today's game between the Spartans and Ducks. He watches ESPN's popular Saturday morning college football show, *College GameDay*. Mostly, he tries to relax.

"Calling a game is a little like taking a test," says Davis—and he has been studying all week. During the week, he has watched tapes of both teams, listened to press conferences, and spoken with both head coaches. By game day, he knows that it is too late to cram.

Another part of Davis' routine is a conversation with Rob Reichley, who is a producer at RayCom Sports. "We don't work together, but Rob is a good friend and one of my true mentors in the business," says Davis. "This is part of the routine."

Davis then puts on his suit and heads over to the stadium. He arrives at least three hours before kickoff for every game. Upon arrival, he makes a beeline directly to the production truck, where the show's producer, director, and technical crew will work the game. The truck is located just outside the stadium.

The people in the truck perform vital jobs, but without fanfare. They are like the stage crew of a theatrical production. Davis visits them to let them know he appreciates the work they do.

"I'm trying to be a man of the people," says Davis. "The more I can show them that I'm on their team, the more they'll be on my team once we hit the air."

Next stop? Upstairs to the broadcast booth, where Davis lays out the tools of his trade: laminated **depth charts** that include a note of interest about "ninety-five percent of the players." Davis also has compiled a list of about three dozen "story lines," or points that he hopes to make during the game if there is time. He distributes the list to all of his teammates in the truck and to his partner, Johnson.

Charles Davis (left) and Gus Johnson are a team for FOX Sports, just like the college football teams they cover.

"After that's done, I like to head down to the field and just get a sense of it," says Davis. It's still 90 minutes before kickoff, and the stadium is relatively empty. Davis knows better than to approach head coaches in these moments, as they are intensely focused on preparing for the game. However, he finds that assistant coaches and other team officials are happy to chat. The information he gathers will help him in his job.

"I don't ask them any questions about the game," says Davis. "The funny thing is, if I don't ask them about the game plan, then they'll tell me."

Davis is highly personable and has a good sense of humor, which helps him to navigate such situations. An assistant coach approaches and asks him to "say something good about me today."

"What if your running back fumbles five times?" asks Davis with a smile. "What should I say then?"

It's time to head back upstairs to the booth, which is located in the press box area. Davis and Johnson do what are known as "pregame hits," video segments in which they converse with FOX's studio hosts on air. They run through their pregame opening as a rehearsal, discussing topics they've agreed upon the night before. Then, as Davis says, "It's time for kickoff, and let the fun begin."

Davis, like most football announcers, stands throughout the game. He finds that it helps him to maintain his energy level. He wears an earpiece, known in the business as an **IFB** (Interruptible Foldback), so that the producer in the truck and sometimes a few other people may converse with him. The fewer voices in his ear, Davis finds, the better.

As Johnson describes the action on each play, Davis provides information on players, such as Heisman Trophy candidate Marcus Mariota of Oregon. His task is to inform viewers while making it also sound conversational. Davis also has to be aware of when the drama of the game takes precedence.

"Somebody once advised me," he says, "that the first three quarters are for storytelling and the last quarter is for coaching. In the fourth quarter, my job is to help viewers understand what both teams need to do, or are trying to do, in order to win."

On this September day, the Ducks prevail. Davis takes the IFB out of his ear and loosens his tie. There's another game next Saturday, but for the next few hours, he can relax.

Words to Understand

articulately: spoken clearly

assess: examine evidence to make a decision or come to a conclusion

investigative reporter: a journalist who focuses on large stories with many parts, interviews, or areas of interest

mimicking: copying

Getting Started

When he was a senior at Syracuse University in upstate New York, Bob Costas (pictured at left) looked and sounded like a high school freshman. Then Costas, who wanted to be sports broadcaster, heard about a job that was opening in St. Louis. The Spirits, a basketball franchise that was part of the old American Basketball Association (ABA), were looking for someone who could do radio play-by-play of their games.

Costas decided to send in an audition tape of himself calling a basketball game. The only problem was that the young Costas had not called a basketball game in two years, and the quality of the recording he had of that game was not very good. So Costas rerecorded the broadcast in his room, editing out the rough patches and even adjusting the bass and treble so that he sounded older.

Comfort in front of the camera is key for any future broadcaster. You need to be able to handle the camera's eye on you at all times.

It was an ambitious, if not completely honest, ploy—but it worked. More than two dozen Emmy awards later, Bob Costas has worked World Series games, NFL playoffs, NBA Finals, and the Olympics. He is one of the most revered voices in all of sports broadcasting. The hardest part was just getting started.

The Basics

Sports broadcasting requires a particular set of talents, and not everyone possesses it. First, it helps to have what is known as a pleasant-sounding voice. While that is not an absolute requirement, it certainly helps. Second, you must understand and appreciate that anyone can read or say words out loud. A good sports broadcaster is also someone whose company the audience enjoys.

Picture yourself on a road trip, taking a long drive across an open highway. That sports broadcaster calling the Cubs-Cardinals' baseball game is your only company. Do you want to listen to him or her for the next two to three hours? Would someone want to listen to you that long? That is a good test for how to evaluate a sports broadcaster's talents.

Sports broadcasters perform many different roles. There is the play-by-play person, who informs radio listeners and/or TV viewers what is taking place. There is the in-studio anchor, who provides the sports news of the day on a local station or a major cable sports network such as ESPN or FOX Sports 1. There are sideline reporters and analysts and investigative reporters and field reporters.

While the particulars of their jobs are different, all of them share a few skills. They speak and communicate well, or **articulately**. They have a presence, either orally or visually or both, that an audience finds captivating. They also think of themselves, to a degree, as performers. When the camera or the microphone turns on, they are "on" as well. That's why sports broadcasting is such an exciting—but often stressful—career.

"When I was eight, my mom died and my dad put me in theater therapy, and he put me in sports to help me cope," says

Lisa Guerrero, a sportscaster who has worked for both ABC and FOX. "I grew up loving sports and performing in school plays. I didn't realize it at the time, but it was preparing me for my future career."

At Edison High School in Huntington Beach, California, Guerrero also read the morning announcements over the intercom during homeroom each morning. "We had about four thousand students, so in the beginning I was nervous," says Guerrero, who is now an **investigative reporter** on the syndicated news program *Inside Edition*. "But then I began to put my personality into it, and it was a lot of fun. It was like doing a news broadcast every morning."

Don't Be Afraid

Most kids and teenagers are afraid of speaking in public, and you may be, too. Public speaking is a huge part of a sports broadcaster's job, though. Like most skills, the only way to improve at it is by doing it over and over.

"Any public speaking is good experience," says Tim Bourret, who has called more than 1,000 basketball games as the color analyst at Clemson University in South Carolina. "When I was a high school student in Connecticut, I did the public-address announcements for our football and basketball games. It was a chance for me to be professional in front of the public."

Some high schools and even middle schools offer classes in speech or rhetoric. Most high schools have a debate team or a speech team. As for those oral reports that your teacher forces you to do in front of the entire class? All of the above provide excellent experience and training.

Tim Ring, an Arizona sportscaster, spends hours preparing his three-minute nightly reports.

"If you're a studio anchor, you also have to be able to write," says Tim Ring, the sports director at KTVK-TV3 in Phoenix, Arizona. "That's the guts of the job. Don't let anyone tell you different."

Nothing is as valuable, or as telling, as self-motivation. Bourret's college roommate at the University of Notre Dame was Ted Robinson, who now is the play-by-play announcer for the

Baseball fan? Take a recorder to the game and call the action from the stands.

San Francisco 49ers. When Robinson was a boy growing up in New York City, he would retreat to his bedroom and watch New York Knicks basketball games with the sound off. Robinson would supply his own play-by-play by speaking into a tape recorder so he could play it back later and **assess** his performance.

"Ted was always trying to improve," says Bourret. "When we were in college, he would attend Chicago White Sox games and sit in the outfield bleachers. The White Sox were not very good at the time, so the crowds were sparse. Ted and a friend would call the entire game into a tape recorder. They could speak as loudly as they wanted because there were so few people sitting near them."

In other words, Robinson was doing play-by-play for free. Now he is paid very well—and has better seats—to do the exact same thing.

Know Your Stuff

If you ever have had to do an oral report, the better you know a topic, the easier it is to speak about it in front of a roomful of strangers. The more passion and interest you have in a subject, the less self-conscious you are. Stage fright disappears if you have confidence. So, if you aspire to be a sports broadcaster, an interest in sports is essential. Your keen interest and passion naturally will lead you to learn as much about it as you are able. It will never feel like a chore.

"My dad taught me how to keep stats when I was ten years old," says Bourret, who also has been the sports information director at Clemson for decades. "We used to sit at the kitchen table in the fall and listen to the Notre Dame football games on the radio. He gave me a long sheet of paper and showed me how to track the game on one area of the paper and keep the individual stats for the Notre Dame players on the other part."

From there, Bourret's father got baseball and basketball scorebooks for his son and taught him how to keep score for each. "I would keep stats on all the games I watched on TV. I did that through middle school and high school. On February 21, 1970, Kentucky played LSU in basketball. Pete Maravich scored sixty-four points for the Tigers, and Dan Issel scored fifty-one for the Wildcats, and I kept score as I watched. I still have the scorebook."

That passion was a sign Bourret was destined for a career in sports. Most play-by-play broadcasters, particularly in baseball, know how to keep score. All of them rely heavily on stat sheets in the same way a doctor relies on lab tests to determine a patient's condition. Learning to keep score of a baseball or basketball or football game, or learning how to read a golf scorecard, is another essential step in your development as a sports broadcaster. It isn't particularly difficult, but it allows you to speak the language of the sport that you are covering.

Find Role Models—but Be Yourself

If you have a favorite team, then you may also have a favorite sports broadcaster. He or she may be the same person who does play-by-play for your favorite team. Maybe you are a big fan of one of the ESPN *SportsCenter* anchors—they always appear to be having so much fun with their jobs. You may even find yourself **mimicking** their style as you call games inside your head or pretend to make that buzzer-beater when you are shooting baskets alone in your driveway.

Don't feel embarrassed: Everybody does it.

While it is fine to have a role model in sports broadcasting (or in any endeavor), it also is important to realize early that the best person to be when you are "on air" is yourself.

Reporters have to learn how to interview people to draw out the best answers for the audience.

"I cannot emphasize enough that the only way to have a long-lasting career in broadcasting is to be genuine and authentic," says Guerrero, who has been reporting in front of the camera for more than two decades. "Be yourself. You can't compete with somebody else by being somebody else."

Talk about your own style: TNT's Craig Sager is legendary for his array of colorful sports coats.

Develop your own style, but that style, like a good pair of sneakers, must fit comfortably. Craig Sager, a basketball sideline reporter for Turner Sports, is renowned for wearing outlandishly colorful suits. Players used to tease him about it, but Sager has always felt comfortable dressing like a peacock. It seems natural to him, so viewers and listeners know that he is not being a phony.

As your personality and identity develop, you should

tailor that identity to the type of sports broadcaster you hope to be. Do not overthink it. If it feels natural, then that's probably the best way to be on air.

First Jobs

What classes or extracurricular work should you do in high school? It never hurts as a broadcaster to be able to write well, so English and writing classes are recommended. Most broadcasters who narrate highlights, such as the men and women of ESPN's *SportsCenter*, write their own "copy." For them, writing well is an essential trait.

It never hurts to audition for a school play, either. You don't have to be the lead or sing a solo, but being able to stand on a stage in front of an audience and perform—to understand what it takes to be "on"—is a skill that you must have for your job.

"A good broadcaster has to bring an extra amount of energy," says Guerrero. "You're not just speaking, but you are 'punching' certain words or phrases—emphasizing them. You may not even realize a broadcaster is doing it when you listen. You only notice how bad it sounds when someone doesn't do it."

Most colleges have campus radio stations, and many have TV stations as well. Understand that you are not going to do play-by-play of the football games as a freshman. Start at the bottom and bring enthusiasm to whatever assignment you are given, even if it seems far from what you want to be doing.

"Always be willing to do the menial jobs," says Bourret. "And it never hurts to learn how the equipment works, or how to edit video or audio. You'll be working with technical people who are behind the scenes your entire career. Maybe you will find you prefer being a cameraman to being on camera. Even if you don't, you'll be better at your job if you understand what it takes for your colleagues to do theirs."

Pursue an internship at a local TV or radio station. "Just go out and get it!" says Allison Hayes, a reporter for the Big Ten Network. "Do some research on stations that will be a good fit for you, and then reach out to the sports director and introduce yourself. Go out of your way to be useful. Never show up late and never ask to leave early."

"Go out and get it!" agrees Ring. "And wear a suit! I went for an internship at WGN in Chicago in 1989. There were twenty-five of us trying to land one job. They gave us a sports quiz. I was later told I was the first person ever to get a perfect score on the quiz. But they also told me that it made a difference that I was one of the few who wore a suit.

"And once you land that internship, don't wait to be asked to do things. Engage. Jump in. Ask questions. Offer to do more. One thing I've found out about professionals: We're happy to help, but it's up to the intern to initiate the process. If an intern is enthusiastic and aggressive, he or she will get what she wants."

If what you want is a career in sports broadcasting, those are all pretty good ideas on how you can get to a place in front of the cameras.

Text-Dependent Questions

1. What does Tim Ring say an anchor needs to do as well as talk?
2. Where did Tim Bourret practice his play-by-play skills?
3. What does Lisa Guerrero say it is important to be?

Research Project

It's never too early to start. Most families now have video cameras, and most smartphones have video and audio recorders. Calling your first game is no further away than hitting the mute button on your TV set the next time your favorite team is playing, and speaking into the audio recorder on a smartphone. Or you can videotape yourself doing it. You could even post the video on YouTube—although you may want to wait until you polish your act a bit.

Words to Understand

producer: behind-the-scenes organizer of a TV broadcast

rundown: the list of individual stories that will make up a sportscast

telegenic: attractive in front of a camera

teleprompter: a device broadcasters watch while reading their script

Hard at Work

Each morning, Tim Ring arrives at work knowing that he will be the star of four two-minute shows later that day. When he sits down at his desk, Ring, the sports director at KTVK-TV3 in Phoenix, has no idea what he will say on the air.

Today, like most days, is a busy one. The NBA's Phoenix Suns are playing in Orlando against the Magic, and the Arizona Diamondbacks are playing their first game of baseball's spring training. The other major professional team in town, the NFL's Arizona Cardinals, just released one of its most popular players of the past decade, defensive lineman Darnell Dockett.

"First thing I do, I read everything that I can get my hands on," says Ring, whose career path has taken him from Green Bay to Miami to Denver and now Phoenix. (Ring's wife is a news anchor at another Phoenix station.) "Time out the broadcast, compose a **rundown**, write scripts, view highlights—all before

A teleprompter works by scrolling the script for the broadcaster. Tags in the script show who is talking (example of "Valerie" above). The script scrolls as fast as the broadcaster can talk clearly.

hitting the set for one of my four sportscasts per day." Some of those terms may sound foreign to you, but we will explain them.

Over the next eight or more hours, Ring will work with a **producer** to create that evening's sports segment of the TV3 newscast. Timing out the broadcast involves deciding how much time, down to the second, to devote to each story. The rundown is the order in which the stories will appear.

Ring also must write scripts for each story so that his words can be loaded into the **teleprompter**. When Ring speaks on-camera, he is reading from the teleprompter, which is why studio broadcasters never seem to stumble over words when addressing the TV audience. The trick is to not make it look as if you are reading.

As a local sports anchor, it is Ring's responsibility to concentrate on the Phoenix-area teams, but he must always keep in mind that day's one or two major national stories. It is a balancing act every night. As airtime speeds closer and closer, it is absolutely vital for Ring and his producer to work quickly and not to panic. Having a great sense of humor, which Ring has, also helps.

"Technical difficulties are bound to happen," says Ring. "The teleprompter stops working or someone puts in a highlight out of order. You have to stay calm and remember that it's just sports."

Have a Routine

The most successful athletes maintain a strict pregame routine: steps they take to prepare for every game that you'll never see on television. For instance, Kyle Korver of the NBA's Atlanta Hawks, the most accurate three-point shooter in the NBA during the

2014–15 season, actually does three different shooting sessions on game days.

Sportscasters are no different from the athletes whom they cover. They, too, find that success comes from establishing a routine that works and sticking to it. "Before I call a game, I start by reading the game notes of both teams," says Clemson basketball radio analyst Tim Bourret. "I pick out a few keys to the game and write them down. I make sure I have the pronunciations of all the players correct, because I can be sure that someone listening will know if I mispronounce a name."

Brent Musburger, one of the most renowned broadcasters of the past 30 years, still attends game-day shootarounds for college basketball games that he calls for ESPN. "It doesn't matter who's playing or where they are ranked," says Musburger, who is in his mid-70s. "Attending the shootaround allows me to talk informally to the coaches in a relaxed environment. And it also lets them know that I care. You build trust that way."

"When I worked at *Monday Night Football*, I'd keep a file for each game or event," says former sideline reporter Lisa Guerrero. "I'd print out stories, read and highlight them, and then I'd make a five-by-seven index card for every story that I thought we might be able to do for that game. For one game I'd print out thirty cards, even though I knew they might only come down to me five or six times."

The Fields of Play

Sports broadcasting is divided into two realms: in-studio and in the field. In-studio includes anyone from the anchors you watch on ESPN's *SportsCenter* to the sports anchor on your local news broadcast. In the field takes in everyone else, from the announcers who do play-by-play and color for games to reporters who conduct interviews after practice.

Sportscasters have to go where the games are—in this case, balancing on the ice awaiting an interview.

Each particular role in sports broadcasting requires a slightly different skill set besides the basic talents that all sports broadcasters must have— the ability to speak clearly and communicate well and with conviction.

Studio anchors, such as Ring, must be able to write well and work with grace under pressure. Field reporters must be ready to appear on camera and remain composed under every type of environment imaginable—poor weather, crazed fans storming a court or a football field after a big win, and a coach or athlete who does not want to cooperate. No matter the circumstances, field reporters have to remain calm.

"It's live television in front of a national prime-time audience," says Guerrero, who'd have to grab a coach or player for an on-field interview immediately after the clock struck 0:00. "It's survival of the fittest."

The challenge of working in the field is that you can rarely control your environment—and you almost never get a second chance. "I had to do a show once from an NFL game, and as I spoke I'd hear myself speaking on a three-second delay in my earpiece," says Ring. "So I'd be hearing the words I'd just said a few seconds later as I was trying to speak. That can be very distracting."

In-studio work has its challenges, too. "Whenever a sports anchor is narrating game highlights," says Guerrero, who used to do updates for FOX Sports, "he or she is reading off what is known as a 'shot sheet.' That's a piece of paper on which someone has written the plays and players who appear on the highlight. As an anchor you have to look at the shot sheet while keeping one eye on the highlights that the audience is viewing. There's an art to it, and it usually takes a lot of practice."

Sports broadcasters are often **telegenic** (that is, good-looking), but there are tricks to looking even better on-camera. "You always have to carry some powder," says Ring. "High-definition television shows every pore on your face, and the lights in the studio can get hot. If you sweat on camera, you look too shiny. The powder hides that. Even guys have to wear makeup in sportscasting."

Being a sports broadcaster means that you are more visible than most media. That has its benefits and its drawbacks. "You have to accept early on that not everyone is going to like you," says Bourret, who is a very likeable

TV reporters such as CBS Sports' Jenny Dell combine good looks and talent.

fellow. "You may make an honest criticism of a team, but a fan of that team may take it personally. All you can do is be honest."

"Don't be arrogant," Ring says bluntly. "If you want people to tune in to see you night after night, state an opinion so that even if someone disagrees with you, they still like you. Remember that the teams and players are the story, not you."

Guerrero discovered that athletes are often fans, too. She liked to use her celebrity to obtain interviews with some of the notorious athletes of her generation, then she'd ask them challenging questions.

"I interviewed Barry Bonds [pictured at left] one-on-one at the height of his steroid controversy," she says. "So many reporters were afraid of Barry and, to be fair, he could be surly around them. I just approached the interview straight on. I asked him the questions that the people at home would ask if they had the chance. I think he appreciated that."

Text-Dependent Questions

1. What is a rundown?

2. What do anchors call the paper that lists highlights they'll be narrating?

3. Makeup for everyone on camera: yes or no?

Research Project

Watch a local sports broadcast and take a lot of notes. Record it if possible to make it easier. Break down the sports segment into the rundown. Which items ran in which order? How long did each item take? Why do you think the anchor chose that order? Would you have done a different order?

Words to Understand

gaffe: a mistake while speaking on the air

Realities of the Workplace

CHAPTER 3

Most days, Tim Ring's young children are more likely to see him on television than in person. Five days a week, Ring, the sports director at KTVK-TV3 in Phoenix, heads out to work at about the same time his son and daughter are finishing their school day.

"You work nights in this business," says Ring. "I work from 2:30 P.M. to 10:30 P.M., Sunday through Thursday. I'll occasionally have to work a Saturday. And I usually work either Thanksgiving or Christmas so that our weekend sports anchor will not have to work both."

The Show Must Go On

There are college and NFL football games on Thanksgiving. NBA games are played on Christmas Day. With the exception of a few

Covering college football such as this game means weekends away from your family.

days before and after the Major League Baseball All-Star Game each July, big-time sports never take a day off. The same holds true for sportscasters. Whenever and wherever a major sporting event takes place, someone is broadcasting it, and sports anchors in studios are reporting on it.

The reality of sports broadcasting is that if you have a job, there are likely at least a hundred people who covet it. Not only does being a sports broadcaster appear to be a glamorous way to earn a living (and mostly it is), but also it is a well-paying job. So you never complain about what days you have to work or what events you might be missing. The job, with the rarest of exceptions for family issues, comes first.

"You will miss important dates and events in the lives of the people closest to you," says FOX Sports football analyst Charles Davis, who had to miss his oldest child's college graduation in order to cover the NFL Draft. "It's unavoidable. You need the understanding of your loved ones to get the job done without added guilt. Just about everything takes a back seat to the job."

Marv Albert, one of the most prolific and successful play-by-play men in television history, chose as the title of his memoir, *I'd Love To But I Have to Work.* That is a sentence that every employed sports broadcaster has uttered at some stage of his or her career.

"I have worked every night, weekend, and holiday for my entire adult life," says Allison Hayes, a field reporter at the Big Ten Network who has also been a local studio anchor. "I have missed lots of weddings and family gatherings, and I am always at a football or basketball game on Saturdays for half the year. But that is to be expected, especially when you are starting out in your career. When you are in your twenties, plan on this being your life."

Job Security

In live television, unemployment is always as close as your next and/or first on-air **gaffe**. All it takes, especially at the outset of your career, is one regrettable comment or a mistaken use of profanity—thinking that you were off-the-air is not an acceptable excuse—to derail your career.

An infamous on-air "blooper," or mistake, happened a few years ago in North Dakota. A news anchor, just 22 years old, was about to be introduced before his first broadcast. Feeling stressed out, he uttered a profanity just seconds before what he thought was the start of the newscast. The problem is that the show had already begun and the young man's "mic" (short for microphone) was "hot," or on.

"If you are wearing a mic, always assume someone is listening," says former FOX Sports and ABC reporter Lisa Guerrero. "The consequences of saying something that you can never un-say are too dire to ever tempt fate."

Reporters and broadcasters learn to treat every microphone they hold or wear as "hot," or actively recording. It helps them avoid saying something that should not get on the air.

A verbal blunder is one way to lose your job in sports broadcasting . . . and fast. The truth is that job security is always an issue on broadcasters' minds. Like coaches on the professional level, sports broadcasters have high-reward, high-risk jobs. Coaches have to win in order to keep their jobs. Sports broadcasters have to win viewers in order to keep theirs. Every television show, especially local news broadcasts, measures its success in large part due to its ratings, which is a measure of

Lisa Guerrero had to overcome some prejudice and harsh words to succeed as a woman in sportscasting.

how many viewers are watching. The more viewers a broadcast has, the more a local station, or affiliate, is able to charge for commercials that air on the network. Hence, the more viewers, the more profitable a network is.

"You earn a spot in front of the camera because someone at the station or network believes you have earned it or that you belong there," says Hayes. "You keep that spot because the public agrees with your boss. If they don't want to tune in to watch you, it doesn't matter how good you think you are at your job."

Double Standard

The first time Lisa Guerrero strolled through a Major League Baseball locker room, she heard players making crude comments about her. She was embarrassed and hurt. Then Guerrero's cameraman at KCBS 2 in Los Angeles nudged her and said, "Watch this."

The cameraman hoisted his camera on his shoulder, flicked it on, and panned the locker room. Every last ballplayer stared at the floor and went mute. "You see, Lisa?" the cameraman told Guerrero. "*That* is the power of the media."

While Guerrero learned an invaluable lesson about the power the media has, she also learned that women sportscasters are judged differently than their male counterparts. "Athletes judge us differently," says Guerrero, "but so do viewers, colleagues, and even bosses. You have to have thick skin, but only figuratively."

It's not fair, but it is reality: Women are judged by their physical appearance far more than men are in sports broadcasting. Fans can and will say mean things to female sportscasters, either in person or on Twitter. Even when they are trying to be nice, like when a Chicago Blackhawks' fan told local reporter Sarah Kustok, "I'm in love with you," while she was interviewing him, it can be awkward.

Physical appearance matters for most sportscasters, men and women, although play-by-play men and analysts are rarely on camera, and for them it matters less. Still, being telegenic plays a role in people watching. It's just that it seems to matter a lot more for women attempting to break into the business than it does for men.

"There is still a massive double standard against women," says Charles Davis.

Competition

There is some good news out there, though. Sports are becoming more popular, and televised sports even more so. When many people whom you see on sports broadcasts were born, ESPN did not yet exist. Neither did FOX, not to mention FOX Sports 1. Nor did the Golf Channel.

In recent years, both CBS and NBC, networks of long standing, have launched sports-specific cable channels. "There are as many jobs in sports broadcasting as there have ever

Everybody wants the interview: This crowded scene is not unusual at big sports events. The demand for sports news is huge; the fight for it can be tough.

been," says FOX's Davis, the former college football player at the University of Tennessee.

Davis waited 11 years after his graduation to enter the business. "I was so stupid to wait so long," he says. "It's what I always wanted to do."

Because sports are so popular, more young people than ever before hope to pursue careers in sports broadcasting. The competition is still fierce, but there exist more places to simply get your foot in the door. As of the beginning of 2015, there were 210 media markets in the United States. That means that even the smallest market (Glendive, Montana) has someone who is a sports broadcaster.

"Somewhere there is a place for someone who is willing to work hard at the start of their careers," says Davis. "I've met young people in the business who say, 'They don't pay me enough' to do such and such. And it's true, at the start they don't. But if you have that attitude, they never will."

Creating your own broadcast is another way to go. If your school does not have a sports broadcast system—such as radio or TV—you can easily find ways to put such a broadcast on the Internet. Talk to your athletic department. If you volunteer to do the work, they might give you a chance.

If you're out of school and looking in the job market, find a place that needs someone who is willing to listen, then learn and outwork everybody. That place exists, and it's a great place for you to start a career.

Text-Dependent Questions

1. In what state does the author set a story about a sports anchor swearing on the air?

2. If you cover the NBA, might you work on Christmas?

3. True or false, based on the text: Women are treated fully equally in sports broadcasting.

Research Project

The author writes about market size. Find out what size the market you live in is. What other markets are nearby you? Can you identify the top ten TV markets in the United States?

Words to Understand

copy: the broadcasting term for the words written down by an anchor to speak on TV

package: a pretaped and pre-edited video segment that runs during a live broadcast

rouge: a makeup product that adds a slight reddish or pinkish tone to the skin

The Nitty-Gritty

When Allison Hayes was starting out as a weekend sports anchor in South Bend, Indiana, her news director called her into his office to offer some advice. "He told me that I was doing a great job," Hayes, now a reporter for the Big Ten Network, says, "but he said I needed to wear less rouge on my cheeks because they looked too red on camera."

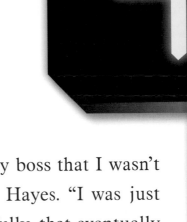

CHAPTER 4

It might have been a helpful suggestion but for one problem. "I had to admit to my boss that I wasn't wearing any rouge," says the fair-skinned Hayes. "I was just blushing because I was so nervous. Thankfully, that eventually went away."

The essence of being a sports broadcaster is live performance. Whether you are simply a voice on the radio or a visual presence on television, you must learn to eliminate that blush.

Even if it is not visible to the audience, viewers can sense it if you are nervous.

"The best way to avoid being nervous," says Charles Davis of FOX Sports, "is to be well prepared. The last thing I do before the red light [the light above the camera] goes on is take a huge, deep breath, choke down my panic, and let my mind go blank. My preparation always brings it back to me."

Before TV people such as ESPN's Rece Davis (left) and Jalen Rose go on the air for a few minutes' work, they spend hours in preparation.

"Prep work is the key," agrees Tim Ring, the sports director at KTVK-TV3 in Phoenix. "If you've prepared well, then by the time the camera is on you, the work is already done."

What exactly, though, is the work?

Writing

Not all sports broadcasters need to be good writers, but many are. Play-by-play announcers, color analysts, and sideline reporters—people who cover live events—do not need to write for television. They react to what they see and report on live events. Everything they say, they think of right as they say it.

However, studio anchors—people such as Ring or the men and women who anchor ESPN's *SportsCenter*—do write **copy**. Most anchors write their own copy. Almost always, when you see an anchor on camera or if you are watching a pretaped "**package**," the anchor has written that copy. That copy has a style unlike a term paper or book report.

"You have to write in short sentences and use action verbs," says Ring. "Even a one-word sentence works. Try closing your eyes the next time you hear a sportscast and just listen to the words. You'll notice we keep it short and punchy."

Talk the Talk

Let's take a look at some key words in sports broadcasting:

IFB: The term is an acronym for Interruptible Foldback and is more commonly known as an "earpiece." Almost every person you see on television wears one. It allows the producer to speak to the person on camera. What most viewers never realize is that a producer is often talking to the person on camera as he or she is speaking or listening to someone provide an answer. Good producers know to speak only when necessary.

"I travel with sets for either ear," says Davis. "You have to think of an IFB the same way you might a pair of eyeglasses or shoes. You're useless without it."

B-Roll: This is footage that is pretaped and accompanies a story. If you are running a feature on, say, female MMA fighter Ronda Rousey, the B-roll might be video of her bouts, or perhaps it would show her training. The sportscaster's job as the B-roll airs is to provide copy that goes with the footage. It's another situation in which good writing matters.

Package: A package is a pretaped segment that runs during a broadcast. For example, during a pregame NFL show, you may see a story on the best catches made the previous Sunday. That will be a package, and it will include plenty of B-roll.

A package is an opportunity for a sports broadcaster and a producer to make a short documentary film.

Stand-Up: Stand-ups, or "remotes," involve anything that is shot or recorded away from the studio. You can think of the difference between stand-ups and studio work as the difference between grilling in the backyard as opposed to cooking in the kitchen. Cooking out can be more fun, but there are also more potential hazards.

Stand-ups often are done live, but some are prerecorded. Live stand-ups, such as when the studio "throws" to a reporter at the scene, are exciting but filled with potential dangers. First,

It might be cold at this ski event, but the reporter doing a stand-up has to smile for the camera as he makes his report.

you are speaking without a teleprompter. A good reporter will jot down a sentence or two, or memorize a couple of lines. Then he or she will rehearse a half-dozen or so times in front of the camera before going on air. Why? Because once the camera is on you and you are live, any number of mishaps might occur (a fan jumps into the shot, or a celebrating player douses you with Gatorade). It is vital not to be distracted. Rehearsal is key.

A live broadcast might include just about anything—even being caught in a Gatorade shower.

"I love doing remotes," says Ring. "It's a great chance to get out of the office. But you're often flying blind. Lots of things can go wrong. Your IFB can go out so that you cannot hear the studio talking to you. You may think you're on camera when you are not. Or vice-versa. There may be a time delay so that what is showing on screen to the viewer is not what you see. The important things are to stay calm and, if all goes wrong, maintain a sense of humor."

"For a live sports event, we usually open with a stand-up, even if we are actually sitting down in the booth," says Davis. "The stand-up is the first and best chance you have to sell the game, the pertinent stories, and yourself."

"The stand-up is the bridge between the studio and the story itself," says Ring. "We introduce the story in the studio, and then we go directly to the reporter in the field for a stand-up. The field reporter provides more detailed information, then we air the story [more B-roll]. And after the story runs, we return to the reporter for a closing word as a bridge to return us to the studio. The stand-up gives us a presence at the story outside of the studio."

"Most of my job involves stand-ups," says Hayes, who for years did stand-ups from Friday night high school football games in Indiana, in all types of atmospheres and weather. "The key is to remain focused and attuned to the studio. It may be chaos and mayhem all around you, but you can't panic. Never let 'em see you sweat."

Behind Every Great Sportscaster . . .

Airplane pilots have air-traffic controllers. Broadcasters have producers. They are the people who work behind the scenes, people whose names you never learn and whose faces you never recognize. Without producers, though, the broadcast would never happen.

An airline pilot must possess a certain skill that few possess in order to fly a plane. However, without an air-traffic controller, he or she would run the risk of having an accident or getting lost. Likewise, a producer surveys all of the other "traffic" out there while allowing the sports broadcaster to do what he or she does best: speak on camera.

Producers remind broadcasters, by speaking to them through their IFB, how much time they have left in a segment before a commercial. Producers listen to an anecdote a color analyst provides, and then provide a graphic or photo that

Producers work in a control room to organize a broadcast and choose which shots go out live.

further illustrates the point. Producers hold meetings before every *SportsCenter* to discuss the rundown of that night's show. They also hold a meeting afterward to discuss what went right or wrong.

"Producers are like the coaches in our field," says Davis. "They call the plays, they coordinate the offense. They do all the managing of the game so all we have to worry about is playing. They are indispensable."

You may decide to pursue a career in sports broadcasting because you like sports. You may have a favorite broadcaster or two. Once you see what the field is like firsthand, you may find that you may like being a producer better. You will never be recognized at a restaurant, but there is something very satisfying about holding so much responsibility in your hands.

Of course, at the other end of every sports broadcast is a person like you, catching up on sports news or watching the big game...and maybe dreaming of being inside that TV someday.

"Some people are born to play the violin," says Ring. "Others are born to conduct the orchestra. There's room for both types in sports broadcasting."

If you know sports, if you love sports, if you can talk well in public and like telling stories, sitting in front of a camera or mic might be your ticket to the big games.

Text-Dependent Questions

1. What is a stand-up?
2. What does a producer do for a sports broadcaster?
3. What goes on B-roll?

Research Project

The author included a handful of broadcasting terms. See if you can find more that he didn't write about. Look online for definitions of terms such as bumper, breaking news, drive time, live-on-tape, VO, and simulcast.

Find Out More

Books

Fuller, Linda. *Sportscasters/Sportscasting: Principles and Practices.*
New York: Routledge, 2008.

Smith, Curt. *Pull Up a Chair: The Vin Scully Story.*
Baltimore, Md.: Potomac Books, 2010.

Zumoff, Marc and Max Negin. *Total Sportscasting: Performance, Production, and Career Development.*
New York: Focal Press, 2014.

Web Sites

ESPN Careers Page
espncareers.com/

Find places to study sports broadcasting
educhoices.org/ (search "sports broadcasting")

Sportscasters Mentoring Group
www.sportscastingcareers.com/

Syracuse University Newhouse School
newhouse.syr.edu

Series Glossary of Key Terms

academic: relating to classes and studies

alumni: people who graduate from a particular college

boilerplate: a standard set of text and information that an organization puts at the end of every press release

compliance: the action of following rules

conferences: groups of schools that play each other frequently in sports

constituencies: a specific group of people related by their connection to an organization or demographic group

credential: a document that gives the holder permission to take part in an event in a way not open to the public

eligibility: a student's ability to compete in sports, based on grades or other school or NCAA requirements

entrepreneurs: people who start their own companies

freelance: a person who does not work full-time for a company, but is paid for each piece of work

gamer: in sports journalism, a write-up of a game

intercollegiate: something that takes places between two schools, such as a sporting event

internships: positions that rarely offer pay but provide on-the-job experience

objective: material written based solely on the facts of a situation

orthopedics: the branch of medicine that specializes in preventing and correcting problems with bones and muscles

recruiting: the process of finding the best athletes to play for a team

revenue: money earned from a business or event

spreadsheets: computer programs that calculate numbers and organize information in rows and columns

subjective: material written from a particular point of view, choosing facts to suit the opinion

Index

Credits

About the Author

John Walters is a senior sportswriter at *Newsweek* magazine. He previously worked at NBC Sports, where he was the recipient of two Sports Emmys for Olympic coverage, and at *Sports Illustrated*. He is the author of *The Same River Twice: A Season with Geno Auriemma and the Connecticut Huskies*.